Hammock Weaving:
The Two-Shuttle Method

Carl D. DuBois

Resource Publications
An imprint of Wipf and Stock Publishers
Eugene, Oregon

Resource Publications
An imprint of Wipf and Stock Publishers
199 West 8th Avenue, Suite 3
Eugene, OR 97401

Hammock Weaving: The Two-Shuttle Method

ISBN: 1-59752-439-5
Publication Date: November, 2005.

Hammock Weaving: The Two-Shuttle Method

Contents

Acknowledgments

I made my own hammocks for 25 years before I finally read a book about hammock making. I learned a few things from that book and wish to acknowledge its helpfulness to me.

The Cofan Art of Hammock Weaving, by M. B. Borman. International Museum of Cultures, Publication 25. (1992) ISBN: 0-88312-185-9. Copies may be obtained from:

International Museum of Cultures
7500 West Camp Wisdom Road
Dallas, Texas 75236 USA

Telephone: (972) 708-7404
Facsimile: (972) 708-7433
E-mail: <Academic.Books@sil.org>
World Wide Web: <http://www.sil.org>

The only other hammock-weaving book I know of is out of print. It is: Andrews, Denison: *How to Make Your Own Hammock & Lie in It*, Workman Publishing Co. (May 1973). It describes in detail how to make four different kinds of hammocks. It describes a fifth, the Mayan Yucatan hammock, but does not tell how to make it. Instead it says, "Instructions on how to make a Mayan hammock would be too complicated for this book...." But I wrote my instructions before I knew it was too complicated to do so.

My thanks to Ray Pittman, whose questions inspired me to write this book.

An invaluable resource on the subject of knot making is accessible on the World Wide Web at http://www.realknots.com.

Introduction

In the mid seventies the Yucatan (Mexico) hammock, made of cotton string, that we had been enjoying began to wear out; strings were breaking that could not easily be pulled back together and knotted. So in 1976 I determined to make my own replacement out of polyethylene fishing line. I examined the weaving pattern of the hammock we had to see how it might have been woven. Then I made my own loom and shuttles and began.

When I began weaving my first hammock, it occurred to me that another cord could be incorporated into the weaving without the need to pass the shuttle separately through the edge of the already woven fabric. It was then that I adopted the habit of alternating between two shuttles, using one for weaving only toward the left, and the other for weaving only toward the right.

Using two shuttles to incorporate a "free" cord into the weaving has the advantage of reducing the time and effort expended by half. But not until mid-2001, when I first read how the Cofan people of Ecuador weave their hammocks, using a single shuttle, did I fully appreciate the significance of the method I had developed. Because of the necessity for Cofan weavers to weave each and every cord separately into the fabric of the hammock, they expend relatively twice as much time and effort as I do to achieve the same result. However, they probably have more time to spend weaving than I do.

Since 1976, I've woven thirteen hammocks purely as a hobby, and at the rate of one about every two years. The hammocks I weave are not for sale. I've resisted offers from those who have wanted to purchase them, but have always been willing to share my knowledge and experience. Over the years, I've taught about thirty others how to weave hammocks using my two-shuttle method. This booklet is an extension of my willingness to teach others how to make their own.

Single Woven vs. Double Woven

Single woven hammock

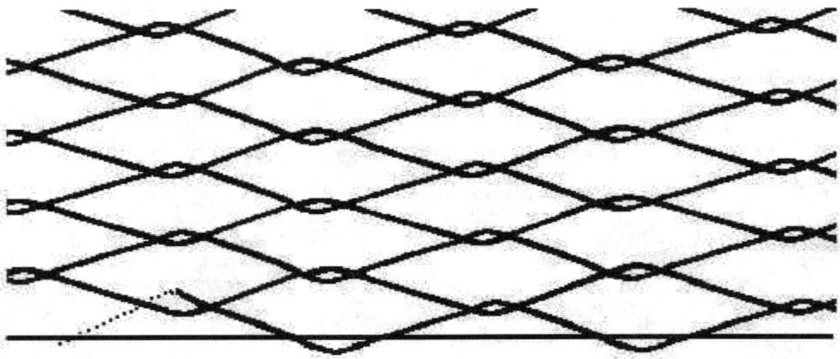

Double woven hammock

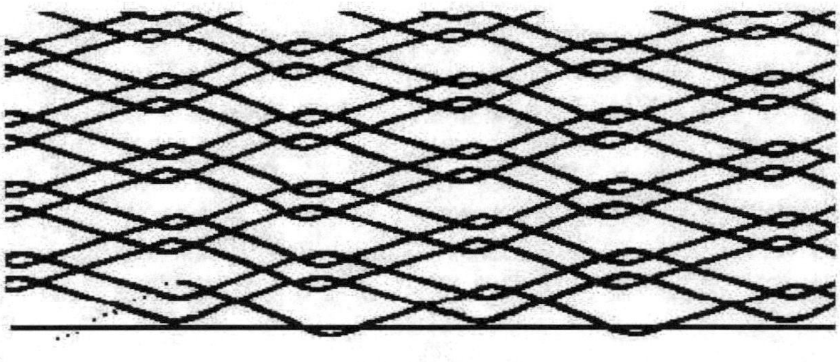

A double woven hammock is like two hammocks interwoven. Because double woven hammocks have smaller holes, they are more comfortable to lie in.

Construction Materials

For the loom:

2 pcs. 1″ x 2″ x 8ft. (horizontal frame)
4 pcs. 1″ x 2″ x 3ft. (uprights)
2 pcs. 1″ x 2″ x 4ft. (long braces)
8 pcs. 1″ x 2″ x 2ft. (framing pieces and bracing)
4 pcs. 1″ x 4″ x 2ft. (framing pieces)
2 pcs. 1″ x 2″ x 6ft. (harness frame)
1 pc. 2″ x 2″ x 24″ (harness frame)
1 pc. 1″ x 6″ x 24″ (humped shape end piece)

1 pc. 1″ dowel or ½″ i.d. pipe 8ft. long (horizontal rod)
2 pcs. ½″ galvanized metal water pipe 24″ long (end rods)

For the shuttles:

6 pcs. 3/16″ x 1½″ x 18″ hardwood (long shuttles)
2 pcs. 3/16″ x 1″ x 9″ hardwood (short shuttles)

Loom Construction

The loom I made and use is eight feet long and 22 inches wide, with a piece of ½" i.d. x 24" water pipe across each end. The loom frame needs to be sturdily made and braced to withstand the tension exerted toward the center.

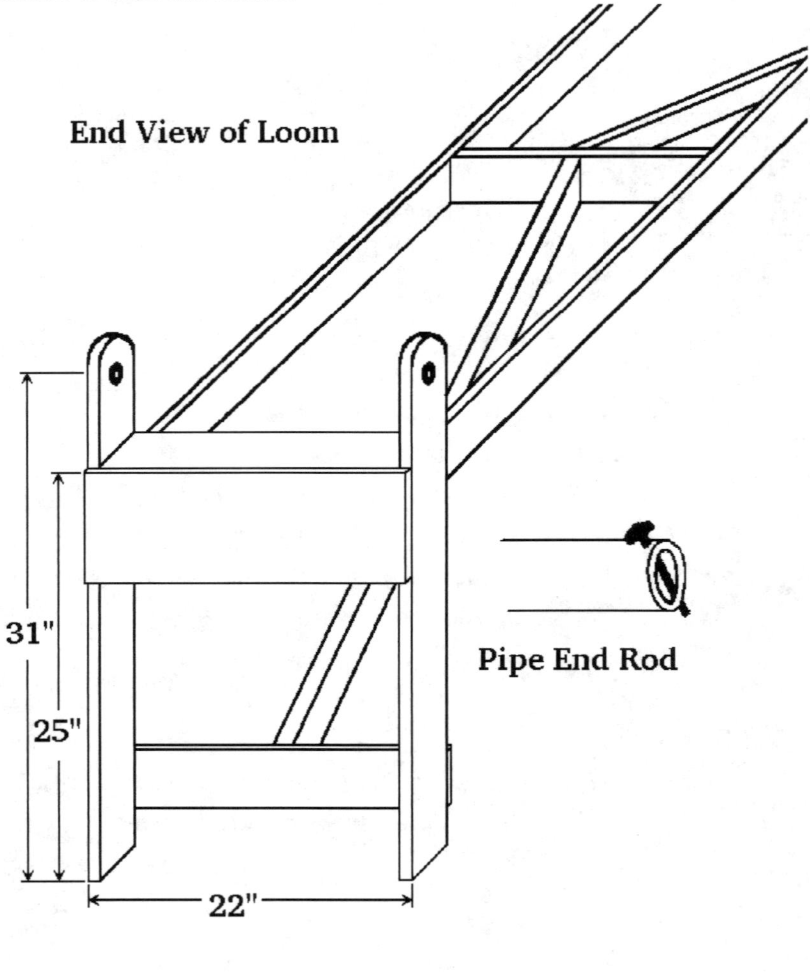

If you plan to weave while standing, you may want to increase all vertical dimensions by 12". For the uprights, make four pieces 1"

x 2" x 33". Round the top ends and drill a hole to accommodate the pipe. Just inside each upright, install the 1" x 2" by 96" horizontal frame piece. Construct the opposite side and other end in the same manner. Nail a piece of 1" x 2″ x 4" wood about 20" long across the tops of the horizontal frame pieces between the uprights as bracing. Nail another piece of 1" x 2" wood between the horizontal frame pieces at the center point of the loom to serve as an anchor for the diagonal braces and a place where the loom may be picked up to move it. Fit two diagonal braces made of 1" x 2" wood between the center wood piece and the bottom cross-pieces at both ends to counteract the tension of the weaving, which tries to pull the top ends together, thus forcing the bottoms of the end frames apart.

The two pieces of pipe are about 24″ long. Drill small holes clear through them within an inch of both ends. Insert nails or small bolts through these holes to prevent the pipes from shifting laterally and coming out of the loom frame.

I usually put a small sign on my loom asking people please not to sit or apply pressure on the weaving, or the frame will break.

Shuttle Construction

I make my shuttles of hardwood, 3/16" thick, 1½" wide, 16" to 18" long overall, and pointed on one end. (See the diagram on the following page.) Round all edges and sand them smooth. Drill a hole through the shuttle through which to pass the end of the cord and tie it to itself to anchor the cord to the shuttle before winding. A coat of varnish may help the shuttles pass more smoothly through the weaving.

I also have a pair of 9" shuttles only 1" wide, which are especially useful when beginning the weaving, and for making the edge cords and end harnesses.

If I use 200-meter (650-foot) rolls, I unwind one roll of cord out 100 meters and back again to locate the center. Then I wind 100 meters on each of two shuttles without cutting the cord at the center. For cord that comes in less than 100-meter (325-foot) lengths, wind a full roll of cord onto each shuttle. When first beginning to weave a new hammock, I recommend using two 1" wide shuttles with not more than 50 meters (150 feet) of cord wound on each one.

While weaving, I like to have several pairs of shuttles wound ahead of time and ready to use.

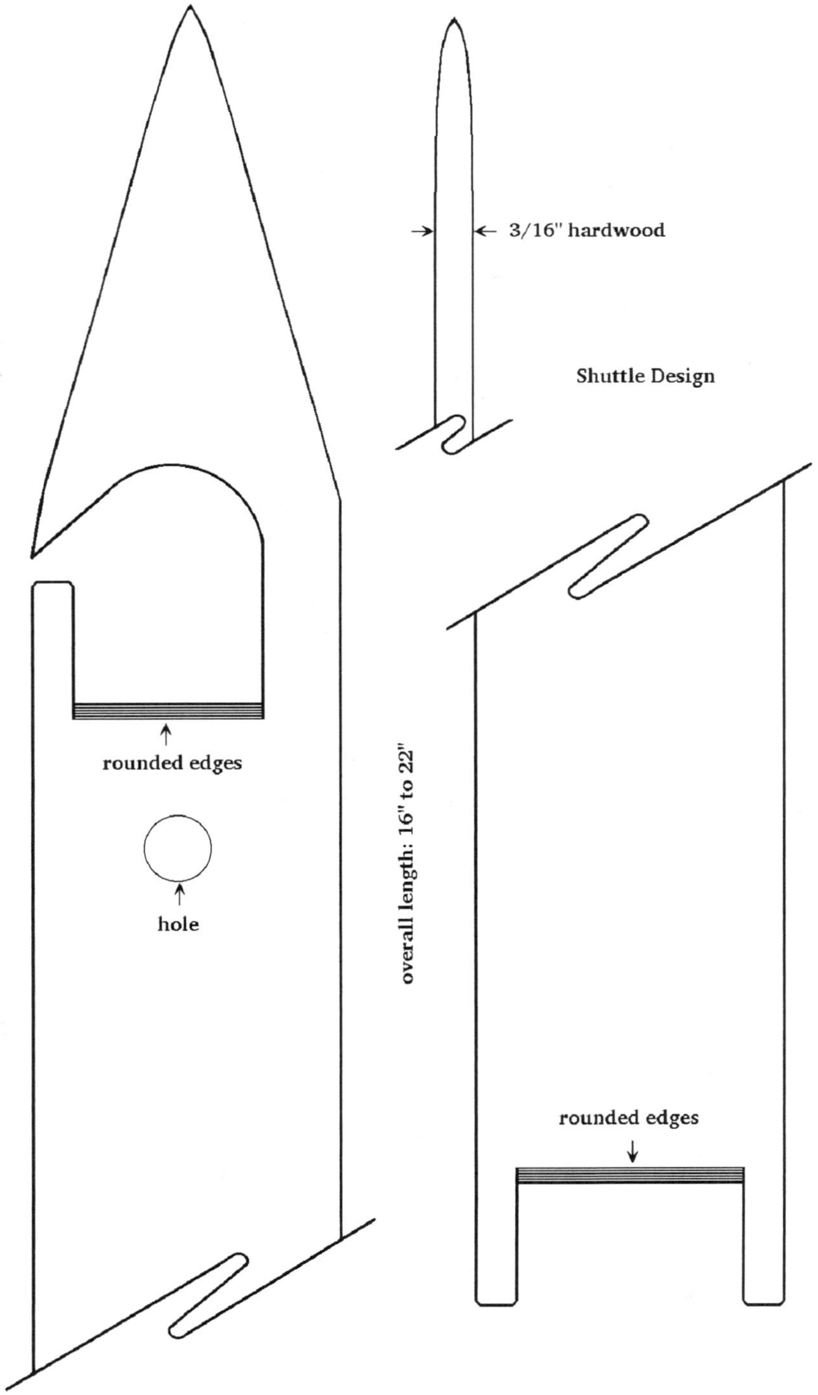
3/16" hardwood
Shuttle Design
rounded edges
hole
overall length: 16" to 22"
rounded edges

Weaving Materials

All my early hammocks were made of polyethylene fishing line. My third hammock was made of very fine #1 (one-half millimeter) fishing line, but because the main section was 80 stitches long, it took a very long time to finish and required more width in order to make it usable.

Beginning with the fourth hammock, all my hammocks have been about fifty stitches long. Until recently I've used nine 200-meter (650-foot) rolls of #2 (1 millimeter) or #3 (1.5 mm.) cord for the center section and edging. The end sections take an additional two rolls of either the same or heavier cord. My last hammock used 45 rolls of number 36 nylon seine twine 36 meters long for the center section, and four more rolls of the same for the end sections. A beginner could get by using 26 of these rolls for the central hammock, and 4 more rolls for the edging and harnesses.

I used to be able to get white polyethylene cord, but have seldom found it in recent years. I've used gold, yellow, and several shades of green and blue, some in combination with white or other colors. I prefer white for the end sections. The nylon seine twine I use now is only available in white, black, and brown.

The cost of materials has been in the range of fifteen to twenty dollars. The labor time might be about sixty-five hours.

Sometimes I've used a pair of two inch welded (and zinc plated) rings to finish off the ends; they are much easier to use than making end loops entirely of cord. They can be purchased at craft or hardware stores. The spare ones I have on hand bear the warning, "Don't use for overhead lifting of a load, support of human weight, athletic or playground equipment."

Getting Started

These instructions are for making a double woven hammock. Place an 8-foot or longer smooth, round rod (1" dowel or ½" i.d. water pipe) lengthwise on top of the loom. Wrap a single cord in a very loose spiral around this horizontal rod the number of times equal to the number of stitches long the central hammock section will be (50 is a good number; 40 is also adequate). It may help if this cord is a different color from the cord that will be used to weave the hammock.

Stretch two strands of colored cord across the loom and tie each one to the end rods; the colors of these two cords should be different from each other (such as blue and red) and different from the color of the hammock (such as white). Tie the ends of the cord on two previously-wound shuttles to each other using a Fisherman's knot. Put the knot on the outside of the right end bar, and unwind cord from one shuttle, moving from right to left. Pass it over the top of the left end bar and let it hang down outside the loom. Then begin weaving with the other shuttle from right to left. Pass the shuttle downward through the first spiral loop, then under and around all three cords: blue, red, and white.

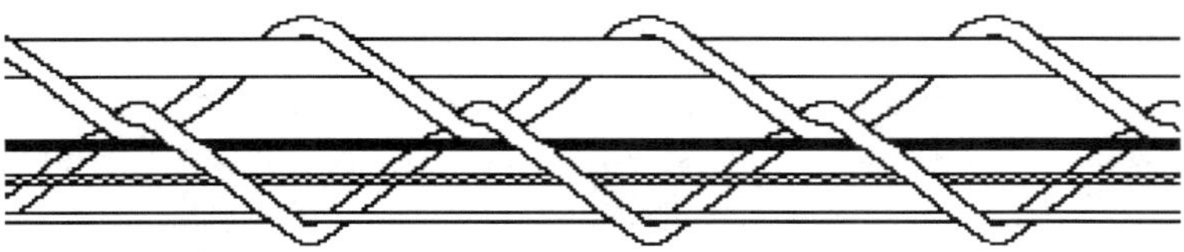

Repeat this action (down through and around) for each loop of the spiral cord until reaching the left end. Then pass the shuttle over and around the left end bar, and unwind enough cord for the shuttle to pass over and hang down outside of the right end bar. This unwoven or “free” cord will be incorporated into the weaving during the next pass.

Make it a habit. when weaving from right to left, to pass the shuttle down through the weaving from the top, and when weaving from left to right, to pass the shuttle up through the weaving from the bottom. If you always pass the shuttle through in the same direction, from the top let us say, the weaving will take on a herringbone pattern.

The next several cords are the most difficult ones to weave because the weaving does not yet lie flat, and this is where the different-colored cords will be helpful. These diagrams are exploded; the actual weaving won’t be so easy to see because the stitches will actually be snugged up more tightly. What is important to remember is always to pass the shuttle around the SAME THREE cords the SAME NUMBER OF TIMES throughout the entire length of each pass. It helps to count stitches.

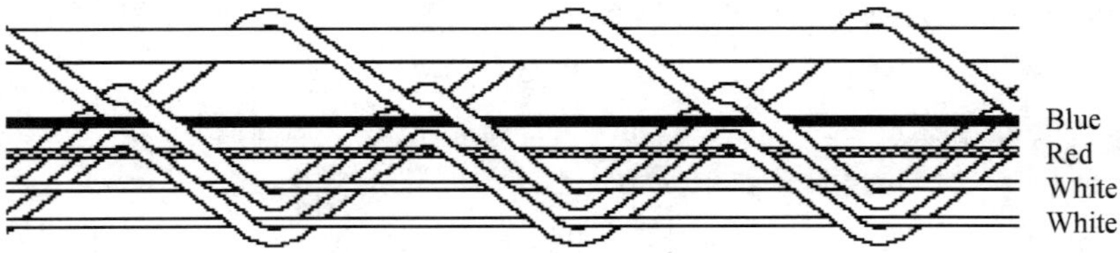

Using the left shuttle, pass it up through and around only THREE cords: the red cord and both white cords. Repeat this action (up through the weaving and around three cords) while moving from left to right, until reaching the right end. Then pass the shuttle over and around the right end bar, and immediately unwind enough cord for the shuttle to pass over and hang down outside the left end bar.

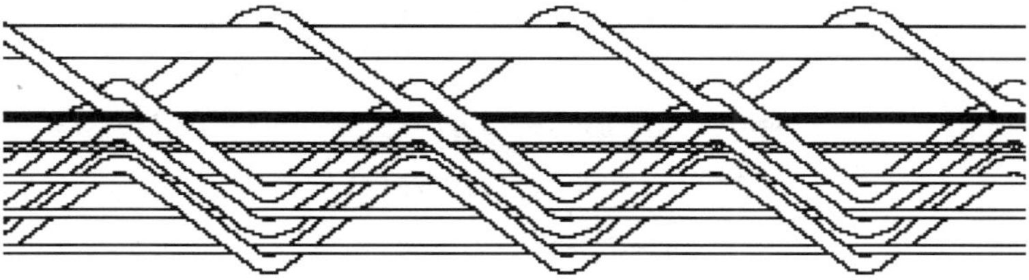

Using the right shuttle, pass it down through and around the three nearest cords, all white: two previously woven, and one "free" cord. By the time this pass is completed, the weaving should begin to lie somewhat flat.

Continue weaving, alternating between the two shuttles.

When the weaving has some discernible width, the loosely wound spiral cord, the rod around which it was wound, and the red and blue cords may all be removed. Then two people can weave simultaneously on opposite sides of the same hammock, if so desired.

Weaving Hints

When starting a new pass, look at the weaving where the second stitch will pass through, and trace the same cords back toward the end to figure out where to put the first stitch through. Special care is also needed when weaving the last stitch of each pass.

Every pass requires the same number of stitches, so I usually count stitches, especially when just beginning. If the count is off, then a stitch was missed, in which case it is better to unweave the stitches and fix the error before moving forward again.

Once the weaving begins to lie flat, the job becomes merely tedious and somewhat boring. You may develop calluses on your fingertips. While weaving I like to scoot back and forth on a bench instead of sitting in a chair. A chair with rollers may also work well. Some people prefer to stand while weaving.

The cord on the two shuttles should run out at about the same time. I've often alternated bands of color across the width of the hammock. Any color and white look nice; two shades of yellow, green or blue also look nice. If using paired shuttles with uncut cord between them, knot the cords to each other at the outside of the end bar. Use only what are called "Fisherman's" knots (see following section). Then put the next pair of shuttles on the loom, unwind one loom length of cord from one shuttle as the "free" cord, and begin weaving with the other shuttle. If using single shuttles, tie the cord from the next shuttle to the end of the cord that is running out. All knots should be on the outside of the end bar, not in the center of the hammock. Leave two inches or more of cord beyond the knots to make it easier to fuse them later.

When weaving the first few rows and before the weaving begins to lie flat, some errors may occur. If these errors are not immediately detected and corrected, you may want to sacrifice the first few rows of weaving at some later time to eliminate the errors.

As weaving progresses, stitches tend to creep in one direction or the other, that is, they may become closely crowded at one end and further apart at the other. The stitches in my own weaving tend to creep toward the right. This can be slowly corrected by forcing the shuttle in the desired direction each time it is passed through the weaving.

Consistency is the secret to weaving superior hammocks.

The Fisherman's Knot

First half of knot:

Complete knot:

The Fisherman's Knot (also called the True Lovers' Knot) consists of a single slip knot tied at the end of each cord. Pull both slip knots tight, and then pull on both cords to bring the slip knots together to form a single knot.

Leave two inches or more of tag end cord beyond the knot to make it easier to fuse the knots with a hot soldering iron. The excess cord will be removed in the process.

When the cord on one shuttle is nearly used up, tie its tail to the cord on the next shuttle if the color will be the same. If you will next weave a different colored band, the tail ends of the first color need to be tied to each other. Knots should be made only at the outside of the end bar, not out in the center of the hammock, where they would be unsightly, and possibly uncomfortable.

Before taking the hammock off of the loom, fuse all knots. Experiment on scrap cord before beginning to work on the hammock knots. Although a soldering iron produces the best appearance, knots may also be epoxied, or fused with a glue gun.

Edging

After weaving the full width of the hammock, I weave a special edging eight cords wide. I suggest using a narrower shuttle with half as much cord as normal. Tie the cord temporarily to the right end bar. Place the knots at every edge stitch. Knots must be spaced evenly on the first pass. To determine this spacing, divide the length (approx. 96" by the number of stitches plus one.

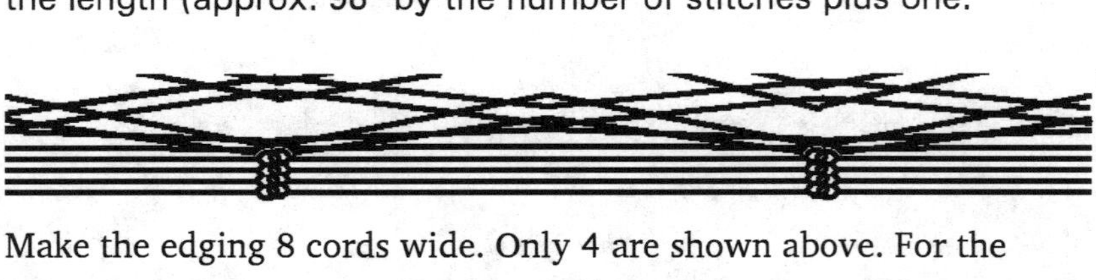

Make the edging 8 cords wide. Only 4 are shown above. For the sake of simplicity in the drawings below, only one pair of intersecting cords (the greyed pair) at the edge of the weaving are shown; two pair would be preferable.

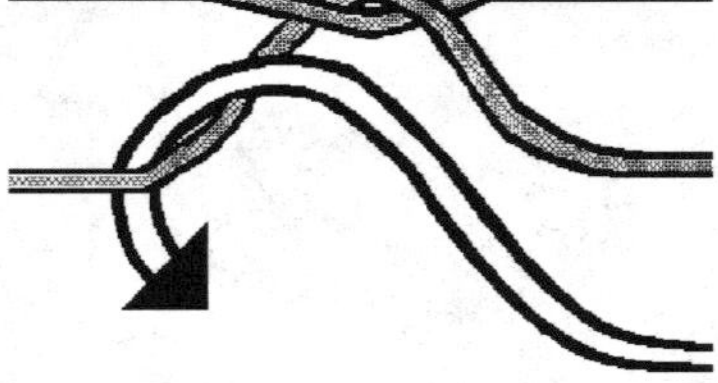

Beginning at the right end, pass the shuttle from the **top down through** the weaving just to the **left** of the intersection where the knot is to be made. Pass the shuttle down through the weaving a second time just to the **right** of the same intersection, and then through the loop that was formed. Check the spacing and then snug the knot tight.

Repeat making knots at the correct intervals all the way to the left end. Pass the shuttle over and around the end bar and begin the second row. Beginning at the left end, the knots are made almost backwards from the way they were made when beginning at the right end.

Pass the shuttle from the **bottom up through** and behind the previous row of edging and just to the **right** of the knot. Pass the shuttle up behind the first row of edging and just to the **left** of the knot, and then through the loop that was formed. Snug the knot tight.

Repeat making knots at the correct intervals all the way to the right end. Pass the shuttle over and around the end bar and begin making knots from the right end, similarly to the knots in the first row.

After the the eighth row is finished, untie the cord from the first row that was tied temporarily to the right end rod, and tie the first and last cords together on the outside of the end rod, using a Fisherman's Knot.

End Harness

Fasten a temporary wood frame to the loom that will hold the terminal ring about 36 inches from the pipe end rod. An end ring is not essential. If none is obtainable, pound a heavy nail into the end piece of the temorary frame and wind the harness cords around it instead of through a ring.

If the end harnesses are made exactly flat, no one will be able to lie in the hammock, because the harness cords going to the sides of the hammock will be longer than the cords going to the center. Therefore, fasten another piece of wood across the width of the loom just outside of the end bar; this piece is in a rounded, humped shape, about 2" or 3" higher in the center than at the ends.

To make the end harness, use the same or heavier cord on a single, narrow shuttle. Tie the free end of the cord to the ring, or make a loop and place it over the nail. Then pass the cord over the humped board, insert the shuttle in the gap that forms just inside the pipe end rod, and pass it under and around eight cords of the central hammock. To avoid shifting of the hammock cords where they pass through the harness loops (resulting in an uneven web pattern), it may be helpful to pass each harness cord twice around each group of eight cords before returning to the end loop or ring.

Then pass the shuttle through the ring (or around the nail) and back to pick up the next eight cords of the central hammock. Be careful not to miss any loops of the central hammock where they pass over the end bar, or they will have no end support. Make the end loop or bind the harness cords together near the end ring (as described in the following text) before making the harness for the opposite end of the hammock.

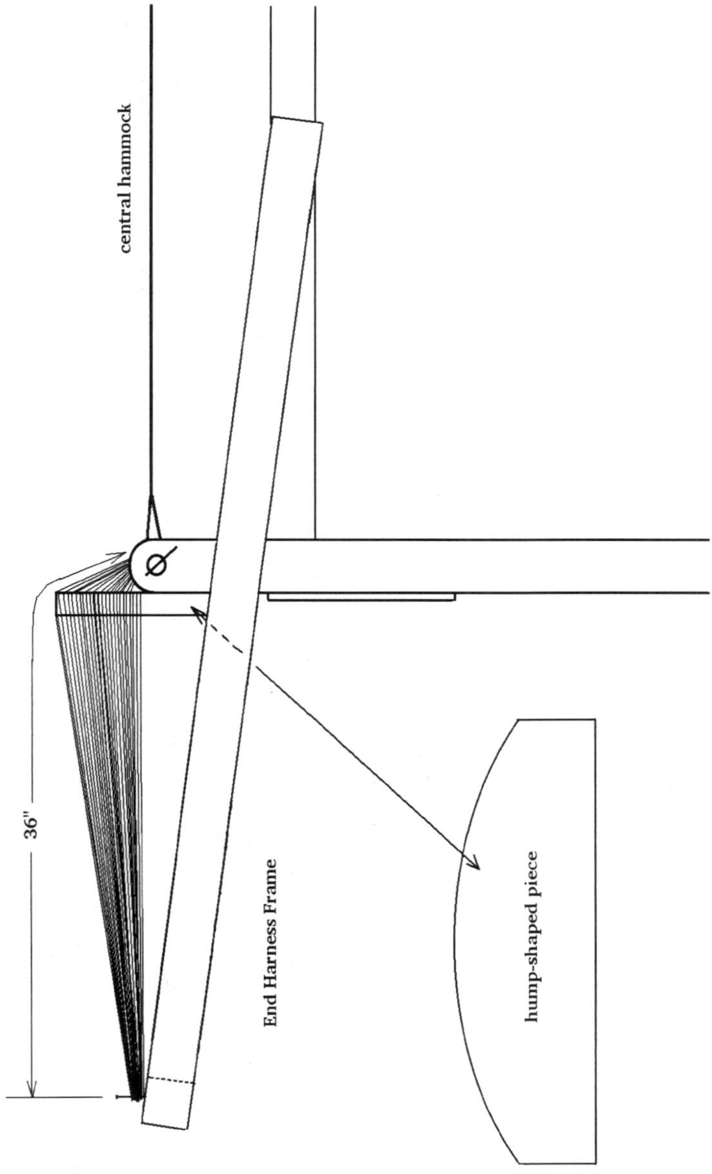
central hammock
36"
End Harness Frame
hump-shaped piece

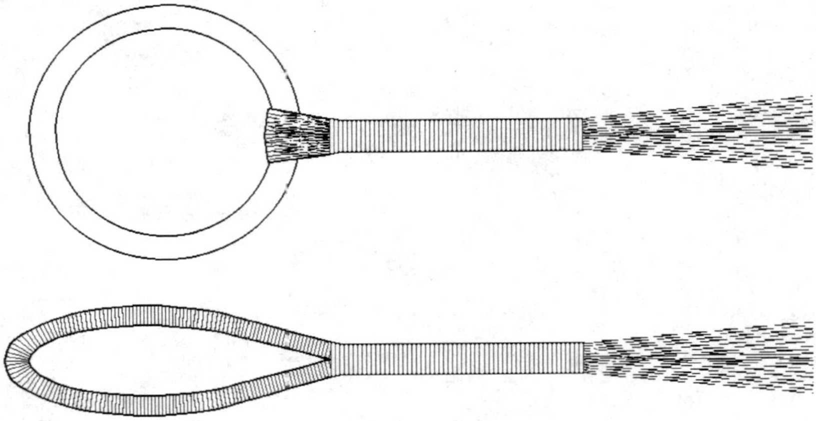

Before removing the harness frame, finish makiing the end loop or ring. When making a bound loop, start wrapping one side of the loop at the bottom, moving up and around to the other side. Then bind all the cords into a single bundle for 3″ to 5″. Before binding this single bundle, lay a tied loop of cord on top of the harness cords and bind it into the bundle.

If using a terminating ring, first lay a tied loop of cord on top of the harness cords. Then tightly bind the harness cords into a single bundle for 3″ to 5″ near the end ring.

When the binding is completed, place the free end of the binding cord into the tied loop. Pull on the opposite end of the loop to thread the free end of the binding cord through the inside of the binding to anchor it. The excess may then be trimmed and fused.

Make the end harness for the opposite end of the hammock and bind its cords in the same manner. Make the harness and loop exactly the same size as the first.

When both end harnesses are finished, remove the temporary framework, remove the nails or small bolts from the ends of the pipe end rods, and push the pipes one at a time out of the frame to release the hammock. If you did everything right, you have the right to feel very pleased with yourself.

BE FOREWARNED. After removing the hammock from the loom, it will be nearly impossible to put it back on the loom again to repair any flaws. The reason for this is that as each strand is woven, it is slightly stretched. After being removed from the loom, all strands return to their untensioned length, and it will be impossible to stretch all of them again simultaneously.

Now make plans to weave your next hammock.

Care Instructions

Before washing a hammock, particularly a nylon one, bind the hammock cords just below the harness loops with a shoe string or other sturdy fabric to prevent the hammock cords from shifting where they pass through the harness loops. NEVER wash the hammock in a washing machine! Try to avoid hand scrubbing to avoid tangling or stretching the cords. Instead, soak it in soapy water for several minutes, then lift it out and back in again several times.

When storing a hammock, avoid tangling by twisting the entire length of the hammock and then bringing the end loops together. If this is done first, the body of the hammock should then coil up all by itself ready for easier storage.

Enjoying

My hammocks are about 14 feet overall in length. They hang very nicely from points about 11 feet apart and about 7 feet high. If to be hung between trees, tie pieces of HEAVY nylon rope to each end loop or ring. If to be hung from wood supports, use eyebolts, split link chain and S-hooks. If a longer space needs to be spanned, extend the S-hooks by inserting welded chain of the necessary lengths.

To be most comfortable lying in a hammock, sit into the center, and then stretch out **diagonally**, with your feet toward one edge and your head toward the opposite edge. That will allow your body to rest in an almost horizontal position.

Denison Andrews, in his book (see the Acknowledgements), describes the Yucatan hammock with the words, "It is as close to flying as you can get without jumping out of an airplane." I'm not really into sky-diving, so I much prefer a hammock.